The United Nations

THE UNITED NATIONS

EDNA EPSTEIN

←—A FIRST BOOK—→

Revised Edition | Franklin Watts, Inc. | New York, 1973

Cover design by One + One Studio

All pictures are published with the courtesy of the
United Nations.

Library of Congress Cataloging in Publication Data

Epstein, Edna.
    The United Nations.

    (A First book)
    SUMMARY: Discusses the purpose of organiza-
tion of the United Nations and describes the work
of its many specialized agencies.
    First-3d editions published under title: The first
book of the United Nations.
    1. United Nations–Juvenile literature. [1. United
Nations]
JX1977.Z8E6 1973   341.23   73-5965
ISBN 0-531-00657-3

Eighth Edition
Copyright ©
1959, 1961, 1963, 1965, 1966, 1968, 1971, 1973
by Franklin Watts, Inc.
Printed in the United States of America
by The Garrison Corp.

FOREWORD

The United Nations is a unique and indispensable instrument for international co-operation in meeting the great challenges of our time. It represents mankind's best hope for bringing about a world of peace, justice and progress.

However, the Organization can be fully successful only if its aims and activities are understood and supported by people everywhere. For this reason, it is very important that there should be continuous efforts to provide accurate and comprehensive information about the United Nations.

This is particularly so today, when the Organization goes through a period of change. Therefore, a newly revised edition of Mrs. Epstein's book is most welcome. It explains the essential facts about the many activities of the United Nations in clear and simple language and shows how the work of the Organization is linked to our everyday lives. In short, it is a valuable introduction to the United Nations and should find a wide audience.

The author's views are, of course, her own.

Genichi Akatani
Assistant Secretary-General
Office of Public Information

Contents

It Belongs
to the World

". . . a part of the United States, belongs henceforth to the world."
So said President Truman on October 24, 1949. It was United Nations Day. The cornerstone of the United Nations permanent headquarters was being laid in New York City.

Eighteen acres of land between First Avenue and the East River in Manhattan make up United Nations headquarters. This land was a gift to the United Nations by John D. Rockefeller, Jr. New York City gave some additional land and the waterfront rights on the East River. It also built the United Nations Plaza.

As President Truman said, the land and buildings of the United Nations *are* international territory. This means that the United Nations makes its own laws for this territory. The United Nations has its own flag. It has its own guards, who police the area. It has its own radio service, which broadcasts in more than two dozen different languages. It has its own post office and issues its own postage stamps.

What Is the UN?

The United Nations is not a nation. Neither is it a world government. It has no citizens and collects no taxes. It has no regular army.

But the United Nations is a great force to keep peace in the world. This is its most important function. It has stopped wars that were already being fought on the battlefield.

The United Nations seeks to raise the standard of living and to better the way of life for people in all parts of the world. This, too, has helped to keep peace.

The United Nations is known familiarly to most of us simply as the *UN*. The cost of the UN to all its member nations is very cheap. The average American pays 30 cents a year, about the price of an ice cream cone. People of other countries pay even less. The share of each country is fixed according to its ability to pay.

In 1970 the United Nations celebrated its twenty-fifth anniversary, with the hope that this birthday would start a period of peace in the world. The theme for the anniversary was "Peace, justice and progress."

UN headquarters, New York.

A general view of the opening of the twenty-seventh regular session of the General Assembly in the Assembly Hall.

Understanding
Each Other

If you were to visit a meeting of the General Assembly of the United Nations, this is what you could expect to see.

More than one thousand men and women would be seated in curving rows in a large, dome-shaped room. These people are *delegates.* They have been sent by their governments to represent them. They come from nearly every country of the world.

Many of the delegates would be wearing earphones that are attached to their seats. They would probably be sitting and listening to a speech made by a fellow delegate.

But if they are people from most of the countries of the world, how can they all understand the delegate who is speaking?

This is made possible by means of the earphones, a six-position switch control, and a special group of interpreters.

The UN has five official languages. These are *Chinese, French, Russian, Spanish* and *English.* If a delegate speaks in any one of these five languages, the interpreters immediately translate the speech into the other four languages. The speeches go into their ears in one language and come out of their mouths in another.

These translations are then carried by wire to the earphones. The listening delegates can follow the speech by tuning in their earphones to any one of the five official languages that they understand.

The interpreter must translate so fast that the speech will sound as if he himself is making it. Besides that, he must make the speech sound as interesting and persuasive as the speaker wants it to be, even if he disagrees with what is being said.

Sometimes a speaker may use a saying that doesn't make sense when it is translated into another language. For example, a Russian may say that an event may happen — "When a shrimp whistles on a mountaintop." He means that it is not likely to happen at all. An English equivalent of this saying is — "When the moon turns to green cheese."

Why is it important for a speech by one delegate to be understood by other delegates from countries all over the world?

It all goes back to World War II.

Working Together
for Peace

World War II was so destructive that the leaders of the Allied Powers felt that some way had to be found to keep peace among nations. In 1945 fifty countries sent delegates to a meeting at San Francisco, where the United Nations was founded. It was organized to handle quarrels between nations that might lead to war.

This was not the first time that nations had decided to work together to prevent war. At the end of World War I, the League of Nations was formed. But the member nations of the League failed to live up to their pledges to take the necessary steps to halt armed attacks.

In 1952 the UN General Assembly met at permanent headquarters for the first time. Lester Pearson of Canada, President of the Assembly that year, in his opening speech compared the tall, high Secretariat building with a "reaching up towards the heavens." The low, spreading Assembly and Conference buildings represented, for him, the need "to keep our feet firmly on the ground." In this way, the very buildings of the UN express the need to be realistic as well as hopeful.

You must have seen pictures of the UN buildings. You may have even taken a trip to the UN yourself. The skyscraper of glass and steel rising sheer and clean from the low-lying buildings at its feet has become as much a symbol of the UN as its blue-and-white flag.

The Charter

The member nations of the UN are bound together by their *Charter,* or constitution. The UN Charter is one of the great documents of history. It has been called an international Bill of Rights. The UN Charter came into force on October 24, 1945. This day has since become known as *UN Day.*

The Charter lays down rules for the member nations to follow. It states the purpose of the UN and defines what the UN can and cannot do.

These are the four main purposes of the UN:

1. To keep peace throughout the world.
2. To develop friendly relations among nations, based on equal rights for each nation and the right of each nation to govern itself.
3. To help improve the living conditions of people all over the world and to promote human rights and freedom for all people.
4. To provide a place where nations may meet together and try to solve their mutual problems.

The membership list is growing all the time. From the original fifty-one members, the UN has grown to over a hundred and thirty.

No nation has to join the UN if it does not want to. Someday, all the countries of the world may be members of the UN.

A meeting of the Conference on International Organization at the United Nations.

The Organs
of the UN

If every nation lived up to the purposes set down by the UN, the world would be a wonderful place to live in. But nations, like people, do not always live up to their ideals.

There are many committees, commissions, and councils in the UN to help carry out its purposes. The Charter itself names only six *principal organs:*

The General Assembly
The Security Council
The Economic and Social Council
The Trusteeship Council
The International Court of Justice
The Secretariat

These six organs, then, help to carry out the main purposes of the UN.

The General Assembly

The General Assembly is the central organ of the UN. All member countries are represented in it. The General Assembly meets regularly each year for a period of about three months. But emergency meetings may be called at any time.

An example where the General Assembly met in an emergency meeting to keep the peace was in the Suez crisis.

The Suez Canal links the Mediterranean with the Red Sea. It runs through Egypt but is used by ships of many nations which would otherwise have to sail all the way around Africa. In July, 1956, Egypt nationalized this Canal, which was being operated by a private French and British company, and announced that Egyptians would run it.

The issue was before the Security Council when, on October 29, 1956, Israeli armed forces entered the Egyptian Sinai Peninsula. Three days later British and French troops landed at the northern end of the Suez Canal. There was great fear that the fighting could cause a larger war.

The General Assembly was called into emergency session. It insisted that Israel, Great Britain, and France stop fighting and withdraw their forces from Egypt. It voted to create a United Nations Emergency Force, called *UNEF.* This force would be made up of troops from the smaller countries. It would not be a fighting force, but a peace force sent with the consent of both sides.

Within a few days, the fighting had been stopped and the first UNEF troops arrived to separate the two sides. Within a few weeks, all the British, French, and Israeli troops were withdrawn.

UNEF troops had taken up positions along the border between

Israel and Egypt and at the mouth of the Gulf of Aqaba, at the southern end of the Sinai Peninsula. As a result peace was restored along the border between Israel and Egypt where scattered fighting had been the rule.

The UN made this peace — which lasted until June, 1967 — with an emergency force of only some 3,000 to 5,000 men. But this small force was backed by the approval, or *moral authority*, of the community of nations in the UN.

The Suez crisis is a striking example of what the UN can do to keep the peace. It shows how mighty is the power of world opinion. For no nation wants to commit an action that will be looked upon with disapproval by most of the other nations of the world.

What Else Does the
General Assembly Do?

The General Assembly is concerned with all the business of the UN. It admits new member nations, on the recommendation of the Security Council. It appoints the Secretary-General, who is the "manager" of the UN, on the recommendation of the Security Council. It elects members of the other organs and watches over their work. It may deal with problems of peace and security. The General Assembly fixes the budget for the UN.

The meetings of the General Assembly are called *sessions.*

Each year, the Assembly elects its own President. Although the Charter does not say so, the President has been chosen up to now from one of the "small" or "middle" powers rather than from one of the Great Powers. The Great Powers are:

China　　　　*United Kingdom*
France　　　*United States*
Soviet Union

If you were to visit a session of the General Assembly, or to watch one on television, you would see three men sitting on a raised platform behind the speaker's stand. The President sits in the middle. The Secretary-General sits on his right and the Under-Secretary for General Assembly affairs on his left.

A matter to be decided upon by the General Assembly is usually put in written form and called a *resolution.* All important resolutions

The Fifth Committee (Administrative and Budgetary) adopts a draft resolution by show of hands.

passed by the Assembly must be approved by two-thirds of the delegates voting.

Each member country has only one vote, no matter how large or small that country is. When a vote is taken, the delegates are asked to vote *for* or *against* a resolution. If any delegates do not want to vote on a resolution, they can *abstain*. This means that they don't vote either for or against. If the vote on the resolution is 40 in favor and 20 against, with 22 abstaining, the resolution would be approved, or what is called *adopted*.

Because the General Assembly has a great amount of work, it usually turns over its problems to various committees first. These committees will discuss the problems and get the necessary information to understand them. Then the committees will pass on their suggestions to the Assembly for it to make a decision.

One important thing must be kept in mind: the resolutions that are finally adopted by the General Assembly are only *recommendations* to the member nations. There is no way of enforcing them by law. But these recommendations carry great weight because the General Assembly represents the voice and public opinion of the nations of the world. In fact, the Assembly is sometimes called the "town meeting of the world."

Delegates
and Delegations

We have said that only nations are members of the UN. A nation can speak or act only through its delegate. Each nation that belongs to the UN keeps a permanent delegation. This is usually headed by an Ambassador, who is the permanent delegate.

Delegates are also called *representatives.* Often, at important meetings, a country is represented by its Foreign Minister or Secretary of State. On some occasions, even its President or Prime Minister may represent it.

Each member nation of the General Assembly votes through its five-man delegation. But it has only *one* vote.

A delegate to the General Assembly has a busy day when the Assembly is in session. The day starts early with a meeting of the delegation itself. Last-minute instructions from the delegate's Foreign Minister are discussed, and plans are made for the day's session. At the end of the day, each delegation sends a report to its own capital.

Political Groups
Within the UN

Voting is never a simple matter of deciding for or against an issue. Nations with similar interests usually vote together. This is sometimes called *bloc voting*.

The *Western Powers* often vote together as a group. These countries are the United States, Great Britain, and some forty nations who are allies of these countries. France often takes a separate line.

The *Eastern Powers* are sometimes called the Socialist States. There are eleven of them. They include the Soviet Union, its allies and Cuba. These countries almost always vote the same way, but sometimes Romania takes a different position.

Then there are the so-called *Non-aligned* countries. These countries are not allied with either the Western or the Eastern powers. There are about ninety of them. Sometimes they vote with the Western Powers, sometimes with the Eastern. On many questions that divide the East and West, they often abstain from taking sides, or they have their own different positions.

There are other, smaller groups. Countries which lie close to each other on the map have many similar interests. These countries are called *regional* groups. Their members hold private meetings to talk about any issues that are important to their region of the world.

The *African group* is the largest of the regional groups. It has over forty members and keeps growing as more and more former colonies become independent nations. The *Asian group* has over thirty members. These two groups sometimes meet together as the Asian-African group. Most of the members are not allied with any of the Great Powers, and these countries are considered non-aligned.

The *Latin American group* consists of over twenty countries of

Central and South America. They are nearly all members, along with the United States, of the Organization of American States.

The *West European and Other States group* consists of the nineteen countries of Europe outside of the Soviet Union and its allies, and includes the United States, Canada, Australia and New Zealand.

On economic and colonial questions, the African, Asian, and Latin American groups usually work closely together. The countries of these three groups are nearly all former colonies and need economic development and assistance. They are nearly all called *developing countries.*

None of these groups has any legally binding organization within the UN. They are not officially recognized as groups. They are called so because most nations that belong to a group usually vote alike. How any group votes will often decide whether a resolution is adopted. No single group is large enough by itself to get a two-thirds majority vote in the Assembly. But the larger groups can sometimes block a resolution by preventing a two-thirds majority vote. So it is necessary to try to work out a compromise, or reach a consensus.

The Security Council

The Security Council was designed to be the main guardian of peace. While the General Assembly deals with all world questions, the Security Council deals only with questions of peace and security. All member nations of the UN have agreed to accept the decisions of the Security Council and to carry them out.

The Security Council originally had eleven member nations, but in 1965 by an amendment to the Charter the number was increased to fifteen. Five of these nations are permanent members. They are:

China   *United Kingdom*
France   *United States*
Soviet Union

The other ten members are all elected for two-year terms by the General Assembly. Five must be from African and Asia, one from Eastern Europe, two from Western Europe and other "Western" states, such as Australia and Canada, and two from Latin America.

The Security Council, unlike the General Assembly, does not hold regular meetings. Instead, it can be called together at any time on short notice. The member nations take turns at being President of the Council for a month at a time.

A general view of the Security Council in session.

Keeping the Peace

After the end of World War II, heavy fighting broke out in Indonesia. This country is made up of a string of islands lying between Southeast Asia and Australia. It had been a possession of the Netherlands for many years. But now it had proclaimed itself an independent republic. The Netherlands did not want to give up her territory. Her army began to fight against the army of the new republic.

The conflict over Indonesia was brought before the Security Council. The Council called for a cease-fire. Then it established a committee to help keep the peace and work out a settlement.

For more than two years, the Security Council worked on the Indonesian case. It urged the withdrawal of Netherland troops and sent military observers to keep a watch on the situation. At times, it had to act to stop fighting that broke out again. It called for the release of political prisoners. The Security Council organized a round-table conference between the countries concerned. Finally it recommended that Indonesia be given its independence and be admitted as a member of the UN.

Throughout this period the Security Council helped to bring delegates of Indonesia and the Netherlands together in the hope of working out a peaceful solution. In this case, as in others, the UN brought the fighting to an end and used its influence to achieve a peaceful settlement.

The Security Council had no armed forces at its command. It sent only a handful of military observers to report on the situation. As with the General Assembly, the Security Council's strongest weapon was the moral authority of the UN.

The achievement of the Security Council in Indonesia is one of many examples of how the UN has helped to keep the peace.

The Veto

Voting in the Security Council is different from voting in the General Assembly. Each member nation of the fifteen in the Security Council is represented by only one delegate and has, of course, one vote.

The delegates sit around a horseshoe-shaped table. On matters dealing with the conduct of business, or how to proceed, decisions are made by any nine states. But on all other matters, the five permanent members must be included in a majority vote of nine. When any permanent member votes against a decision, this is called a *veto*. An abstention is not a veto. When a permanent member is itself involved in a quarrel where force is not used, it cannot vote.

The veto power was put into the UN Charter to prevent the Security Council from making a decision which would endanger the interests of one of the Great Powers. If this happened, it could be very dangerous.

A Great Power cannot be forced to do something against its will. If pushed too far, a Great Power could start a chain of events that might lead to war. The veto is a sort of safety valve to prevent too much pressure from building up against any one of the Great Powers.

All the permanent members of the Security Council are in favor of the veto. None of them would want to give it up. But the Western Powers — that is, the United States, Great Britain, France, and their allies — charge that the Soviet Union abuses the veto power. The Soviet Union, in turn, claims that the Western Powers control a majority of the votes. Thus, they claim, the Western Powers have a "built in" veto.

In 1950, during the war in Korea, the General Assembly adopted a resolution called *Uniting for Peace*. This resolution states that, whenever a veto prevents the Security Council from acting in a case where peace is at stake, the General Assembly can be called into a special *emergency session.*

The first emergency sessions were called in 1956, for both the Suez and the Hungarian crises. Others were called in 1958 over the crisis in Lebanon, in 1960 for the crisis in the Congo, and in 1967 after the Middle East conflict.

Enforcement Action

The Security Council is the only UN organ which has the power to take strong measures, or *enforcement action*, to preserve peace. This enforcement action may be carried out by peaceful means, such as breaking off trade relations. It may also be carried out by military force.

The Charter provides for the Security Council to have an international police force at its call. Since the UN has no armed forces of its own, it was decided that the Security Council would enter into special military agreements with the UN member nations. Under these agreements, member nations would supply troops and military aid at the Security Council's request. However, as the permanent members of the Council could not agree on the kind or number of armed forces each one should contribute, this idea has not been carried out.

In 1950, the Security Council for the first time recommended military action. It recommended that UN members give military aid to South Korea to repel the North Korean invasion, which was done.

Both the Security Council and the General Assembly, however, can create an *international peace force.* A UN peace force can only enter a country or stay there with the permission of that country. The Egyptian government had to give its permission for UNEF to operate there. The Congo government itself asked the UN Force to come to the Congo.

UN Forces on duty in 1960 in Leopoldville, Republic of the Congo.

How the Two Organs
Keep the Peace

While the Security Council is the main keeper of the peace, the General Assembly can also discuss any question of international peace and security and can make recommendations on any such questions.

Thus it is possible for countries to choose whether they want their complaints to be dealt with by the Security Council or by the General Assembly.

Although the Assembly can only make recommendations, while the Council can make decisions which are binding on all UN members, this has made little difference. The moral authority of the UN, the pressures of world public opinion, and the willingness of nations to carry out a UN resolution can make a General Assembly recommendation as effective as a Security Council decision.

Each of these two organs has dealt with many cases affecting peace. A country with a complaint will take it to whichever organ it thinks will deal with it most favorably.

If there is a veto in the Security Council, a case can be transferred to the General Assembly. That was done in several cases.

How a Case
Is Dealt With

A problem can be taken to the Security Council or the General Assembly only by nations, not by individuals. After a country decides to take a case to either of these two principal organs, it asks that the case be put on the *agenda*. This means that the matter will be put down in written form and the organ will decide whether to consider it.

The case cannot be heard until the organ concerned agrees to hear it. After this is done, the delegates of the nations involved present their views. Resolutions that set forth ways of dealing with the case can be suggested by any member nation.

It is not easy to work out a satisfactory solution for most problems. By the time a case reaches the UN, it has a long and complicated background. A case is seldom all right or wrong. It usually must be dealt with in stages, each one requiring a great deal of discussion.

The Importance
of Talk

Sometimes the speeches and discussions seem to go on and on without ever coming to an end. Sometimes, too, the debate is very bitter. However, as a delegate once said, "It is better that elderly diplomats get ulcers in debate than that young men get killed in battle."

Not only does the continual talk allow for a cooling-off period, but the exchange of views is sure to bring to light any opening where helpful action might be taken. By the time some one hundred nations have expressed their views on a given situation, world opinion has emerged. The power of world opinion to influence a country's behavior is very great.

In addition, the time taken up in debate is needed for the countries involved to work out suggestions that might be followed. The delegates must think out each move carefully. They must imagine how it could affect all other situations.

There are many factors to be weighed. There are the views and reactions of all the other UN members. There are the many different pressures on each government, both from citizens at home and from foreign countries. All these make it necessary for every course of action to be carefully studied in detail. The wonder is, not that there is so much talk and that so much time goes by before a decision is reached, but that decisions are reached as soon as they are.

What Can Be Done

There are many courses of action the UN can take.

Sometimes the Assembly merely expresses hope that the nations who disagree will try to smooth out their differences. Sometimes commissions, or committees, are established to carry out all sorts of jobs. They may find out the facts of a case and make recommendations or keep watch over a dangerous situation. They may supervise a truce or make suggestions for a friendly settlement of a disagreement.

Military *observers* may be sent to a troubled area to discourage illegal actions. There they will watch developments and report on them. At different times observers have been sent either by the Council or the Assembly to Greece, Palestine, Kashmir, Indonesia, Korea, Lebanon, and to the Suez Canal.

The countries in dispute may be warned that, unless the resolutions adopted by the UN are agreed to, they might have to be enforced to keep the peace. When fighting is already going on, the first step is to call for a cease-fire.

In the case of the Suez, the Congo and the Cyprus crises, the UN sent emergency military *forces* to keep the peace. In the case of Korea, the UN called on all its member nations to give military and other aid to South Korea. It also asked that no help be given to North Korea and Communist China.

The following member states are inscribed around the plaque:

United Kingdom of Great Britain and Northern Ireland · United States of America · Australia · Belgium · Canada · Colombia · Ethiopia · France · Greece · Luxembourg · Netherlands · New Zealand · Philippines · Thailand · Turkey · Union of South Africa

Unified Command

The United Nations

in grateful remembrance
of the men of the Armed Forces of Member States
who died in Korea
in the service of the United Nations
1950 - 1953

A bronze memorial plaque in the public lobby of the General Assembly building. It commemorates the men of the armed forces of the member states who died in Korea in the service of the UN.

Korea

At the end of World War II, Korea was occupied by American troops in the south and Soviet troops in the north. These troops were stationed in Korea under a wartime agreement. It was hoped that Korea would soon be free and independent.

In time, however, two separate governments developed. They were known as North Korea and South Korea. Under a UN recommendation, American and Soviet troops were to be withdrawn. The American withdrawal of troops was observed by a UN commission; the Soviet withdrawal of troops was not.

In June, 1950, North Korean troops crossed the dividing line and invaded South Korea. Heavy fighting broke out. The Security Council demanded that North Korea halt its attack and withdraw its troops to its own boundary line. When North Korea ignored this demand, the Security Council called on all member nations of the UN to help South Korea against the invading North Koreans.

Some forty countries sent food, money, and other help to South Korea. Sixteen countries sent troops to help defend South Korea. American troops were the first in action and led the fighting against the invader. The United States was put in charge of the combined UN forces. These forces fought under the UN flag.

The UN forces had driven back the North Korean army when volunteers from Communist China joined the fighting on the side of North Korea. The UN General Assembly called on Communist China to withdraw the invading forces.

The fighting continued and reached a stalemate around the original boundary line dividing North and South Korea. Peace talks began in July, 1951, between representatives of the UN forces and those of the Korean People's Army and the Chinese People's Volunteers. Two years later, an armistice agreement was signed.

During the three years of fighting there were hundreds of thousands of casualties — dead, wounded, and missing — on both sides. But the attackers were driven back and South Korea was successfully defended. For the first time in history, an international army had been called into action by a world peace organization to defend a country against an armed attack.

The Middle East: 1947-49

After World War I, Great Britain governed Palestine under a kind of trusteeship agreement. The problem of independence for Palestine was complicated by the quarrels between the two main groups of people living in Palestine, the Arabs and the Jews. Both groups claimed a right to govern the country.

In 1947 Great Britain referred the Palestine question to the UN. The General Assembly decided that Palestine should be divided into two independent countries, one Jewish and one Arab and an international regime for Jerusalem. Boundary lines were recommended.

The Jews in Palestine accepted the UN plan. The Arabs were unhappy with the plan and refused to accept it. Guerrilla fighting began. Neighboring Arab countries said they would send troops into Palestine to help the Arabs there. Jews all over the world said they would help the Jews of Palestine. Palestine seemed on the verge of war.

On May 14, 1948, the British withdrew from Palestine and the Jews declared their independence in the area recommended for them by the UN. They called this new nation Israel. The next day troops from the surrounding Arab nations attacked Israel.

The Security Council took up the case immediately. It called for a stop to the fighting. A truce was finally arranged by the UN. Military observers were sent to Palestine. Fighting broke out from time to time, but the UN always managed to stop it quickly. Finally in 1949 armistice agreements were signed by Israel with the surrounding Arab countries — Egypt, Jordan, Lebanon, and Syria.

Ralph Bunche, an American working in the UN Secretariat, won a Nobel Peace Prize for his efforts in helping Israel and the Arab countries agree on the armistice.

A peace treaty was not signed and shooting sometimes took place along the armistice line. Among the unsettled matters is the question of the Arabs who became refugees as a result of the war in Palestine. These refugees are still living in camps. They are being aided by the UN.

Another unsettled question is passage for the ships of Israel through the Suez Canal. While these ships sail the Gulf of Aqaba, Egypt (now called the United Arab Republic) would not allow them to go through the Canal.

Dr. Ralph Bunche (above) visits the United Nations Emergency Force in Gaza. UNEF troops (below) withdrawing from the Gaza Strip after the United Arab Republic terminated its consent to UN presence.

The Middle East: 1967

As was explained earlier, the United Nations Emergency Force was created in 1956 to stop the fighting in Suez and Sinai. For more than ten years UNEF helped to keep the peace in the area. Suddenly, on May 18, 1967, the United Arab Republic demanded that all UNEF troops be withdrawn from its territory and moved its own troops up to the Israeli border. Thus UNEF came to an end. The United Arab Republic also announced that the Gulf of Aqaba would be closed to Israeli ships and Israel declared this would be a cause of war.

On June 5, war broke out between Israel and the United Arab Republic, Jordan, Syria and other Arab states — the third war between Arabs and Israelis in twenty years. The Security Council, as a first step, called for an immediate end to the fighting. By June 10, a cease-fire had been agreed to by Israel and Jordan, the United Arab Republic, and Syria. During the fighting Israeli forces had occupied the Sinai Peninsula up to the Suez Canal, the part of Jordan on the west bank of the Jordan River and the Syrian heights overlooking the Sea of Galilee and the Jordan River. The Suez Canal was blocked.

The problems of the area were discussed at an emergency session of the General Assembly in June and July of 1967. The General Assembly did not agree on any recommendations for an overall settlement. But it called for fair treatment for refugees, civilians and prisoners of war and called on Israel not to change the status of Jerusalem.

Finally, in November the Security Council unanimously decided that the Secretary-General should send a Special Representative to the Middle East to help to bring about a peaceful solution and a just peace. Since 1967 the Special Representative has been trying to get the parties to agree to a settlement and the United States has tried to get them to agree to open the Suez Canal.

The Congo (Zaïre)

On June 30, 1960, a Belgian colony, the Congo, became an independent state. A few days later the soldiers of the Congolese army mutinied against their Belgian officers. Riots and disorder broke out. Belgium sent troops to the Congo to protect the Belgians there. The situation became very dangerous.

The new Congo government in Leopoldville (now Kinshasa) appealed to the UN for military assistance. The Security Council immediately called on Belgium to withdraw its troops. It also asked the Secretary-General to provide military aid and technical assistance to the Congo government.

The Secretary-General decided not to use troops from any of the Great Powers. He asked African and other smaller countries to provide troops for a UN Force to help the Congo. Within two days troops from five African countries had been airlifted to the Congo. In a few weeks a UN Force of about 20,000 men, mainly from Africa, but coming from 28 states in all, had arrived. They spread out over the huge country to maintain law and order. They were to make sure that the Belgian army left the country. It was also their job to protect the unity and independence of the Congo. As they were a peace force, UN troops would not fight unless they were attacked.

The Province of Katanga proclaimed its own independence from the Republic of the Congo, and allowed Belgian troops and hired soldiers (mercenaries) to stay on there. There was danger of civil war. The Security Council called for the withdrawal of these troops from Katanga and ordered the UN Force to enter the Province. But it took more than two years, until January 1963, before the UN Force got full control of Katanga and its secession was ended.

The Secretary-General also sent many members of the UN Secretariat and from the Specialized Agencies to help the Congo government. These civilians and experts gave technical assistance to the different branches of the Government. The Congolese people had not had enough training or education, so the UN experts were needed to help run the country. They brought in and distributed food. They started up the hospitals and health services again and the airports and air services. They began a program of public works. They helped to get factories and farms and people working again. They helped all the machinery of Government to get going. They kept the country from collapsing.

The Secretary-General called the UN's work in the Congo "the biggest single effort" ever made by the UN itself. In addition to the 28 countries that provided troops for the UN Force in the Congo, many other countries furnished equipment, supplies and services for both the military and the civilian operations. To avoid rivalry among the Great Powers the Secretary-General wanted all military aid for the Congo to be sent only through the UN. A resolution in the Security Council containing this idea and asking the Secretary-General to continue his efforts in the Congo was vetoed. So an emergency session of the General Assembly was called in September 1960 and it approved the Secretary-General's actions. The General Assembly also called on all states again for more money and help for the Congo, but said that military aid should be sent only through the UN.

Secretary-General Dag Hammarskjold lost his life in a plane crash in September 1961 while on a peace mission to the Congo. His successor, Secretary-General U Thant, carried on his work. Finally peace and order were restored and the UN Force was able to withdraw in 1964.

By its great work for peace in the chaotic and violent situation in the Congo, the UN was carrying out its main task to keep peace in the world. It is also helping the Congo to get a good start on its new independent life and to take its full place among the family of nations. In 1971, the Congo changed its name to Zaïre.

Finding a
Compromise Solution

The two main UN organs, the General Assembly and the Security Council, try to find a settlement agreeable to both sides involved in a dispute. When each side agrees to give up some of its demands, this is called a *compromise.*

In the early years of the UN, the General Assembly and the Security Council often formed commissions to try to find a compromise solution. In recent years, the UN has come to rely more and more on the Secretary-General for this purpose.

The Secretary-General can work quietly with disputing delegations behind the scenes. He can also deal personally with heads of governments. In this way, he helped to get American prisoners released who were being held in Communist China after the Korean War. He used his influence directly in the Suez crisis, in the Congo, in West New Guinea (West Irian), in Cuba, and in many other crises, to help reach a peaceful compromise solution.

Disarmament

Both the General Assembly and the Security Council have tried to convince the countries of the world to give up their arms. The Disarmament Commission was created to make plans on how this idea might be put into practice.

One of the principal aims of the UN is to stop the arms race. If countries did not spend so much money on keeping up with each other in developing and producing weapons of destruction, more time and energy and money could be devoted to making a better life for everyone.

From its very beginning, the UN has tried to ban the use of atomic and hydrogen weapons. Also, it has tried to get countries to reduce their armed forces under an adequate system of control.

The problem is a complicated one. Since the national safety of every country is at stake, there is fear and distrust among nations. For any nation that would succeed in hiding and storing its arms while all other countries were destroying theirs would have a tremendous military advantage.

In 1959 Premier Khrushchev proposed to the General Assembly a plan for the total disarmament of all countries. The General Assembly approved the idea unanimously. The UN is trying to find a way to get the nations of the world to agree on a disarmament treaty with effective controls. The Soviet Union and the United States have agreed on a set of principles for total disarmament and a peaceful world.

The Geneva Disarmament Conference is trying very hard to reach agreements on total or partial disarmament and arms control. In 1963 the Soviet Union, the United Kingdom and the United States made a treaty to stop nuclear tests in the atmosphere, under water and in outer space. More than one hundred countries signed the treaty. In the same year the General Assembly banned all nuclear weapons from outer space. This was written into the Outer Space Treaty of 1967. When Pope Paul VI addressed the General Assembly in October 1965 he appealed for "Never again war," and said, "If you wish to be brothers, lay down your weapons."

The UN and the Secretary-General helped prepare the Treaty of Tlatelolco of 1967 which bans all nuclear weapons from Latin America. In 1968 the UN approved the Treaty for the Non-Proliferation of Nuclear Weapons, whose aim is to prevent nuclear weapons from spreading to other countries.

In 1970, the UN approved the Seabed Treaty that banned nuclear weapons from the land underlying the sea. In 1971, it also approved a treaty banning the development and production of biological (germ) weapons, and providing for the destruction of all stockpiles of these weapons.

The UN is trying to get agreement on treaties to stop underground nuclear weapon tests, and to ban all chemical weapons. It also has called for a stop to the manufacture of any new kinds of nuclear weapons. It has declared the decade of the 1970's to be a *Disarmament Decade*, with the goal of achieving as much disarmament as possible in these ten years.

The Secretary-General, with the help of international experts, has prepared four important reports: to show that disarmament would not hurt but would help every country's economy; to explain the dangers of nuclear weapons; to show that all chemical and biological weapons should be completely banned; and to show that the arms race and heavy military expenditures are a threat to human welfare and survival.

Science for Peace

The UN has also taken steps to ensure that modern science and technology are used to help mankind and not to harm it. In 1953 President Eisenhower proposed to the UN General Assembly that, even though the nations had not been able to control atomic weapons, they should try to use atomic energy for peaceful purposes.

In 1957 the UN established the International Atomic Energy Agency. This agency will promote the peaceful uses of atomic energy and help countries to build nuclear-power reactors and to use nuclear explosions for peaceful purposes only.

The UN is also studying ways to see that outer space is used for peaceful purposes. It has approved several treaties dealing with outer space to lay down principles and rules to see that it is used for the good of all countries and peoples. It is trying to do the same for the oceans and the seabed. It is also trying to make sure that modern science and technology will be used to help new countries. Several conferences have been held by the UN where scientists have come from all over the world to exchange scientific information.

It is trying to stop pollution and in 1972 held a world-wide conference on the human environment in Stockholm in order to protect and improve the air, land, and water environment in which we all live. The Stockholm conference adopted a declaration on responsibility for the environment and designated June 5 as World Environment Day; it adopted an Action Plan with 109 recommendations to preserve and improve the environment. The UN set up an Environment Fund and a Council for the Environment Program with headquarters at Nairobi in Kenya.

A technician working at the Belgian Research Center on the Uses of Nuclear Energy.

The Economic
and Social Council

The Economic and Social Council is called *ECOSOC* for short. It is concerned with such problems as jobs for all, trade, education, and health. ECOSOC also works to improve the rights and freedoms of people everywhere.

ECOSOC has done much to help improve the living conditions of people in countries where progress and development have been slow by modern standards. These countries are generally referred to as being *underdeveloped* or *developing*.

There are twenty-seven member nations in ECOSOC. All are elected by the General Assembly for three years. The main decisions in the economic and social fields must be made by the General Assembly, but plans are studied and recommendations made by ECOSOC and its commissions and committees.

To take some examples: the General Assembly set up a *Development Program* to help start important projects in underdeveloped countries. It declared the decade of the 1960's a *Development Decade* to increase the growth rate of all countries and to aim at an annual growth rate of 5% for the developing countries by 1970, and the 1970's as the *Second Development Decade*. During the first Development Decade, the budget for this partnership between the rich and the poor countries increased from about 50 million to 250 million dollars a year. During the Second Decade, it is hoped that this sum will increase to over a billion dollars a year. It created a permanent body called *UNCTAD* (United Nations Conference on Trade and Development) to increase trade and speed up the development of the less developed countries; it also set up another permanent body, called *UNIDO* (United Nations Industrial Development Organization) to promote the development of industries in these countries.

Since 1955, United Nations experts have been helping the Indonesian government develop the country's leather industry. Here Indonesians are at work in one of the modern new laboratories.

Technical Aid

Technical assistance, or aid, was first developed by the UN. It is the sharing of important know-how intended to help underdeveloped countries learn to help themselves. This form of aid has been one of the main achievements of the UN. Because of its great success, technical aid is becoming more popular and is expanding all the time.

All the UN member nations have joined in sharing some of their technical knowledge. Many thousands of experts from more than 100 countries have given their technical skills to more than 125 countries and territories that have asked for them.

Ways of growing crops have been improved. New factories have been built and old ones have been improved to produce more. Public health work and greater child care have been introduced. Advice has been given on better ways to collect taxes and on how to carry on the business of government better. More houses and schools have been built.

This program has meant a real sharing of skills between the countries of the world. Many countries which receive technical aid in one field, such as engineering or government, may send experts in other fields, such as archaeology or fishing, to other countries. No country need feel that it is receiving a handout, for all are working together as members of the UN. And all share in the cost of the technical aid program.

The value of working together for the good of people all over the world cannot be measured, but it is as real as technical aid. The UN has thus not only helped many countries to strengthen their economies and raise their standards of living, it has also helped to make for better relations between countries themselves.

A UN engineer agronomist from Italy discusses ways of improving the barley crop with an Andes Indian in Ecuador.

UNICEF

After World War II, there were millions of children left homeless or orphaned by the war. The UN set up the International Children's Emergency Fund, called *UNICEF*, to help care for them.

So successful was the work that UNICEF was set up as a permanent organization to help needy children — particularly in underdeveloped countries. UNICEF has given food and medicine, clothing and supplies, equipment and training to many millions of children and mothers in over one hundred countries and territories.

UNICEF wages war against diseases that attack children, such as yaws and tuberculosis. Yaws is a terrible disease that causes sores to break out all over a person's body. It can cripple a person who gets it. Yet yaws can be cured by a single dose of penicillin.

UNICEF and the World Health Organization, working together, have made great inroads against yaws in more than twenty-five countries. They have all but ended yaws in Haiti.

UNICEF gets most of its money from governments and individuals. This money is given voluntarily. Some funds come from the sale of UNICEF Christmas cards, which have become popular all over the world.

Children themselves help to raise funds for UNICEF. Many thousands of them in the United States and Canada go out on Halloween with milk containers to collect money for UNICEF in place of the usual "trick or treat."

The work of UNICEF is regarded as so important for peace that in 1965 the Nobel Peace Prize was awarded to UNICEF.

A UN guide, in the traditional dress of her native Ghana, discusses a UNICEF exhibit with a group of school children.

Aid for Refugees

The UN has appointed a High Commissioner for Refugees. This was done to help the millions of people forced to flee from their homes and take refuge in other countries by war or politics. In 1959-60 the UN organized the World Refugee Year to help find new homes for all refugees.

The High Commissioner has given protection to millions of refugees. So highly is its work regarded that, in 1954, the Office of the United Nations High Commissioner for Refugees was awarded the Nobel Peace Prize.

The Office helps the refugees in many ways and tries to find permanent homes for them. After the Hungarian revolt in 1956, the Office gave large-scale aid quickly to thousands of Hungarians who had fled their country. There are very few European refugees at present, but in recent years there has been a large increase of refugees in Africa. In 1971, the UN and the High Commissioner undertook a massive program of aid to the millons of refugees from East Pakistan (now Bangladesh), the largest operation of this kind in history.

A mother and child, two of the many thousands of refugees resulting from the war in the Middle East between Israel and the Arab States.

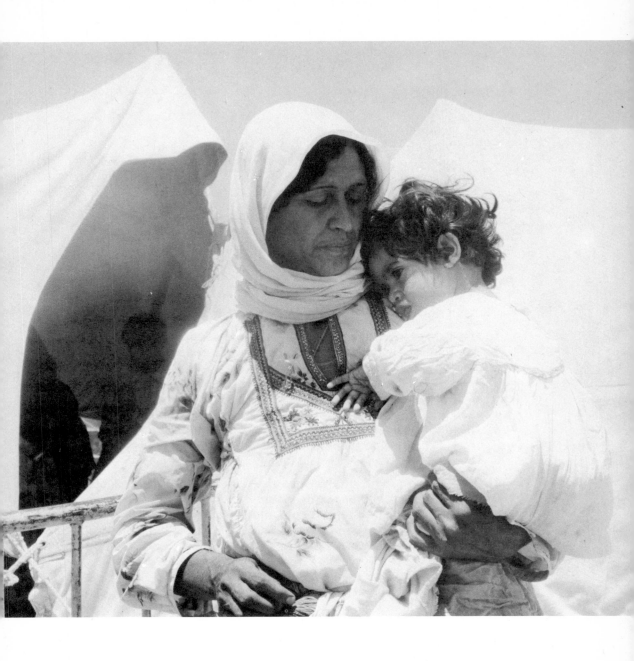

Human Rights

As we have seen, one of the main purposes of the UN is to promote human rights and freedoms. For the first time in history, the UN has worked out an *international* definition of the rights of man. This is the *Universal Declaration of Human Rights.* It was adopted on December 10, 1948. Since then, every December 10 is known as *Human Rights Day.*

The Universal Declaration of Human Rights sets forth the following human rights as goals for all governments to work toward:

1. The right of individuals to life, liberty, and security.
2. The right of everyone to an education and to equality before the law.
3. The right of each person to move about freely, to worship as he chooses, to associate freely with other people, and to have access to information in his search for understanding.
4. The right of everyone to be a citizen of a country, to work under favorable conditions, with equal pay for equal work.
5. The right to marry and raise a family.

The UN also adopted in 1966 two new papers on human rights. They are called *International Covenants on Human Rights*, one on Economic, Social and Cultural Rights and the other on Civil and Political Rights. They are meant to carry out the ideas of the Universal Declaration. In 1967 the General Assembly adopted a Declaration on the Elimination of Discrimination against Women.

The Universal Declaration of Human Rights is one of the finest accomplishments of the UN. It is also a great step forward in the progress of mankind.

This Declaration has played a large part in forming the constitutions of new countries. It has helped to change the views of some countries toward slavery, forced labor, and the rights of woman and children.

The UN is helping to make the standards set forth in this *first world charter of human rights* become actual facts in the lives of people throughout the world.

Racial Discrimination and Apartheid. In recent years the UN has given more and more importance to the problem of racial discrimination which it opposes as a serious violation of human rights. It is studying ways and making recommendations to end this discrimination.

In 1963 the General Assembly adopted a Declaration to eliminate racial discrimination. In 1965 it gave a more legal form to this by spelling out the duties in a treaty called the *International Convention on the Elimination of All Forms of Racial Discrimination.*

One of the most difficult problems in the UN is the problem of "apartheid." This is the name given to the plans of South Africa to separate the races there. There are about 15,000,000 black "Africans" and less than 5,000,000 white "Europeans" in South Africa. The UN has objected to apartheid as being a form of racial segregation and discrimination and for many years has discussed and condemned apartheid and tried to get South Africa to change its attitude. South Africa says that this is an internal matter and that the UN has no right to interfere. The General Assembly has adopted resolutions saying South Africa's policies were a danger to international peace, has called on the UN members not to trade with or help South Africa, and set up a Special Committee on the Policies of Apartheid. The Security Council called for an arms embargo — members are not to sell or give arms to South Africa.

Health and Education

The UN is also working to improve health and to do away with major diseases. The World Health Organization, UNICEF, and the various agencies for technical aid — all are helping to bring some of the world's great diseases under control.

Many widespread diseases are being steadily reduced. Dangerous epidemics have been halted. Malaria, for example, which has killed millions of people, may be totally wiped out in about ten years' time. Leprosy, too, is on the way out.

More than half of the people of the world cannot read or write. The United Nations Educational, Scientific and Cultural Organization was set up especially to help get rid of illiteracy in the world and to improve education and scientific and cultural cooperation between nations. The UN decided to establish an international university.

UN personnel working on the international control of narcotics. By developing and testing methods, the geographical origin of drug samples can be determined through their chemical and physical characteristics.

Groups Within
ECOSOC

The work of ECOSOC is too big for a single organ. It has many commissions to help it with its work. One group is known as the *functional commissions*. Here, each commission deals with a special subject on which it advises ECOSOC. The main functional commissions are:

Commission on Human Rights
Commission on Narcotic Drugs
Social Commission
Population Commission
Commission on the Status of Women
Statistical Commission
Commission on International Commodity Trade

The second group consists of the *regional commissions*. These deal with the special problems of different geographical areas.

The regional commissions are:

Economic Commission for Europe (ECE), in Geneva, Switzerland
Economic Commission for Asia and the Far East (ECAFE), in Bangkok, Thailand
Economic Commission for Latin America (ECLA), in Santiago, Chile
Economic Commission for Africa (ECA), in Addis Ababa, Ethiopia

ECOSOC is the only principal organ of the UN that deals with groups not associated with any government. These groups are called *nongovernmental organizations,* or NGOs for short. They consist of private citizens, not in the employ of their governments, who have joined together in societies, clubs, trade unions, and the like. ECOSOC may discuss a particular problem with an NGO to get the benefit of its special knowledge.

The Specialized
Agencies

ECOSOC does not depend on the functional and regional commissions alone to do its work. It also works with what are called *specialized agencies.* These are separate world organizations. They are made up of whichever member nations join them. The World Health Organization is such a specialized agency.

Each agency deals with its own special branch of concern. Its membership is much the same as that of the UN, though some agencies have fewer members and some have more.

While each agency has its own budget and handles its own affairs, it is associated with the UN. The agency and the UN have an agreement which defines how they work together. The agencies can propose matters to be taken up by the UN. They can also send delegates to the ECOSOC meetings.

The agencies, which are all members of the "United Nations family," are:

International Atomic Energy Agency (IAEA), in Vienna
International Labor Organization (ILO), in Geneva
Food and Agriculture Organization of the United Nations (FAO), in Rome
United Nations Educational, Scientific and Cultural Organization (UNESCO), in Paris
World Health Organization (WHO), in Geneva
International Bank for Reconstruction and Development (BANK), in Washington
International Finance Corporation (IFC), in Washington
International Monetary Fund (FUND), in Washington

International Civil Aviation Organization (ICAO), in Montreal
Universal Postal Union (UPU), in Berne
International Telecommunication Union (ITU), in Geneva
World Meteorological Organization (WMO), in Geneva
Inter-Governmental Maritime Consultative Organization (IMCO), in
   London

In 1969, on its fiftieth anniversary, the ILO was awarded the Nobel Peace Prize for helping to improve the living conditions for all working people.

ECOSOC, with its various commissions and the specialized agencies, is the best organization ever set up to deal with the world's economic and social problems.

Promoting
Independence

In the past, new nations were born usually as a result of war. The UN has helped to change this.

When the UN was founded, there were only four independent African countries. Now there are over forty. More than seventy countries in Africa, Asia, and the West Indies have become independent members of the United Nations. Most of these nations have been created by peaceful means. More are on their way to independence.

Here is an example of how the UN works in such matters.

After World War II, the Great Powers could not agree on what to do with the former Italian colonies of Libya, Eritrea, and Somaliland. They referred the question to the UN General Assembly. The General Assembly voted independence for Libya, the joining of Eritrea to Ethiopia, and trusteeship for Somaliland for ten years. Somaliland is now Somalia, an independent member of the UN.

The existence of the UN and its Charter has made it easier for new nations to achieve independence. The work of the UN in helping territories achieve their independence is a part of their program for developing friendly relations among free nations all over the world.

In 1960 the General Assembly decided that all forms of colonialism should be ended quickly, and adopted a Declaration to give independence to colonial countries. It also set up a Special Committee on decolonization to see that the Declaration was carried out. The work of this Committee has helped to speed up the independence of many countries.

Problem Areas in Africa. Some difficult cases in southern Africa have not been settled. *Southern Rhodesia* was a colony of the United Kingdom with about 250,000 white people and about 5,000,000 Africans. In November, 1965, the white minority rebelled and declared the independence of Rhodesia, an act the United Kingdom opposed. The UN condemned it and called on the United Kingdom to put an end to the racist minority government. The Security Council decided that the illegal government should not be recognized and called on all states not to give it any help or supply arms or oil and to break off all economic relations.

South West Africa had been a Mandated Territory (like a Trust Territory) under the League of Nations. South Africa was the administering power. After World War II, South Africa refused to make South West Africa a Trust Territory under the UN. The General Assembly condemned South Africa's policy of apartheid in South West Africa, and said that South West Africa had a right to be free and independent. In 1966 the Assembly decided that the Mandate was ended and that South West Africa should be directly under the UN. In 1967 it decided that a UN Council for South West Africa should administer the Territory, to be called Namibia, through a UN Commissioner until independence. South Africa has refused to cooperate.

Angola, Mozambique and *Portuguese Guinea* are territories in Africa under Portugal's administration. Portugal says they are not colonial territories but are overseas provinces of Portugal and part of the Portuguese nation. The UN decided these territories were colonies and have the right to be free and independent. Portugal refused to obey the UN requests. The UN called on all Member States not to help Portugal or sell her any arms.

The Trusteeship Council

The Trusteeship Council deals with Trust Territories. These are former colonies now supervised by the UN under the terms of "trusteeship agreements." Each agreement states *who* shall govern the territory and *how* it is to be governed.

The country that governs, or administers, the territory is called the *administering* power. It has to govern according to terms that agree with all the purposes of the UN Charter. The terms must also provide for the progress of the territory toward self-government.

The Trusteeship Council is made up of eight member nations. Four members administer, or govern, Trust Territories. The other four do not. Each member nation of the Trusteeship Council has one vote. Decisions are made by a simple majority.

The Council prepares and sends out questionnaires on the progress of the people of the Trust Territories. It examines petitions, or written requests, from the people of the Trust Territory and makes visits to inspect the territories. Originally there were eleven Trust Territories. Now there are only two — the Trust Territories of the Pacific Islands (under the United States) and the Territory of New Guinea (under Australia). Burundi, Cameroon, Rwanda, Tanzania and Togo are examples of former Trust Territories that are now independent countries.

The Trusteeship Council Chamber.

Non-Self-Governing Territories

The UN not only watches over the Trust Territories. It also watches over the people in *Non-Self-Governing Territories.*

These territories are governed by a country that decides their affairs for them.

But the Trusteeship Council supervises only the Non-Self-Governing Territories that are also Trust Territories. So the General Assembly set up a special committee to watch over the progress of the other Non-Self-Governing Territories. The countries which govern these territories send regular reports to the UN telling about conditions there. The special committee discusses these reports and gives advice to the governing countries.

At first, information was sent on more than sixty territories, but this number is quickly becoming smaller. More and more territories are becoming self-governing. All of them join the UN when they become independent.

An interesting point here is that, in the work concerning Non-Self-Governing and Trust Territories, the UN is putting itself out of business. One day, it may be able to stamp all of its work in this field as "Completed."

The International Court of Justice

Under the UN Charter, nations must settle their quarrels peacefully. The General Assembly and the Security Council help nations to achieve a peaceful settlement of *political* quarrels. The International Court of Justice helps them to settle their *legal* ones.

The Court is the main UN organ for handing down legal judgments. Only nations take part in cases before the Court, and then, only when they choose to do so. Unless both nations involved in a case agree to submit it to the Court, the case cannot be heard.

More than thirty nations, however, have announced in advance that they will take all their legal cases to the Court. Dangerous situations have been smoothed over because of decisions made by the Court.

The Court sits at the Hague in the Netherlands. It is in permanent session. It has fifteen judges. They are chosen not as representatives of nations but as individuals. No two can be of the same nationality. Decisions are made by a majority of the judges, provided at least nine are present. Judgments of the Court are final.

The Anglo-Norwegian fisheries case is a good example of how the Court works. The United Kingdom argued that Norway had no right to close off certain zones along its coast to foreign fishing. The British and Norwegian governments took their quarrel to the International Court of Justice. In 1951 the Court decided in favor of Norway. The United Kingdom accepted the judgment and the case was closed.

In addition to hearing cases between nations, the Court can also give advisory opinions on any legal question when so requested by another UN organ.

For example, some of the members of the UN did not want to pay for the heavy costs of keeping the UN Forces in the Congo and in Suez. So the General Assembly asked the Court for an advisory opinion. The Court ruled that all UN members must pay their share of these costs.

Most nations generally look upon their quarrels with other nations as being political rather than legal. Therefore many more cases are referred to the General Assembly or the Security Council than to the International Court, which, of course, only hears legal cases.

The Secretariat

The Secretariat is the sixth principal organ of the UN. It consists of the Secretary-General and the UN staff.

The Secretary-General is the chief administrator for the UN. It is his job to see that everything in the organization runs smoothly.

The Secretary-General is appointed by the General Assembly, on the recommendations of the Security Council, for a period of five years. He is chosen from one of the smaller nations, because he must not be personally involved in either side of any quarrel.

Trygve Lie of Norway was appointed the first Secretary-General in 1946. In 1953 he resigned and was replaced by Dag Hammarskjold of Sweden. Mr. Hammarskjold was chosen for a second five-year term in 1957.

Dag Hammarskjold died in a plane crash in Africa on September 18, 1961, while on a peace mission for the United Nations.

U Thant of Burma was chosen to succeed Dag Hammarskjold. He was unanimously elected Secretary-General and held that office for ten years (two terms) until 1971.

On January 1, 1972, Kurt Waldheim of Austria took office as the new Secretary-General for five years.

The Secretary-General has been given the same kind of political power in the UN that is held only by nations. The UN Charter states that he can refer to the Security Council any problem which he feels may threaten world peace. He can also propose issues to be considered by the General Assembly and other UN organs.

The Secretary-General is always on hand to assist the members and organs of the UN. The different views of members often make it difficult or even impossible for them to agree. It has become more

and more usual, therefore, for members to ask the Secretary-General's help in touchy situations that call for a great deal of fair play and diplomacy.

The Secretary-General has no interests to promote except those of the UN. He does not play favorites. UN delegates, on the other hand, have to act in the interests of their own countries.

Confidence in the judgment of the Secretary-General has grown over the years. By his practice of quiet diplomacy behind the scenes, he has often been able to work with delegates in settling differences between their countries.

Left, former Secretary-General U Thant. Above, Secretary-General Kurt Waldheim.

International
Civil Servants

The Secretary-General is assisted by an international staff. The staff members are *international civil servants* who must not seek or receive orders from anyone outside the UN.

For their part, the member nations of the UN are bound by the Charter not to attempt to influence the Secretariat staff members in their work.

The Secretariat is chosen on as wide a geographical basis as possible. There are some 14,000 members of the Secretariat. About one-third of them are at the headquarters in New York. The rest are spread all over the world in branch offices, information centers, and on technical assistance and other missions.

The number of its own people that each member nation may have in the Secretariat corresponds roughly to how much money the member nation contributes to the budget. But even the smallest countries are entitled to have up to five of its citizens in the Secretariat.

The work performed by the Secretariat varies from assisting or advising the Secretary-General to guarding the buildings or writing reports for UN organs and committees. The interpreters whom we met in the beginning of this book are staff members of the Secretariat.

Workers for Peace
and a Better World

The Secretariat has sometimes been described as the oil that keeps the machinery of the UN running smoothly. It has also become a sort of storehouse of experience to help the delegations in their work.

In spite of their different nationalities, backgrounds, and outlooks, the staff members of the Secretariat get along together as well as any group of workers in any country.

The international civil servant is a new type of official in the modern world. He works for international peace and a better world in the workshop of all nations. If you include the workers in all UN bodies and Specialized Agencies, there are about forty thousand of them today. There will be many more of them in the world of tomorrow.

The Importance
of the UN

Now you have seen how the UN, through its various organs, achieves its aims. It helps to keep peace, to improve living standards and human welfare, to promote the independence of nations and to improve relations between them.

In the few short years of its existence, the UN has clearly shown how important it is. Peace has been preserved when it looked as if war could not be avoided.

We have seen how the UN helped to restore peace in conflicts in different parts of the world. The Suez Canal crisis in 1956 is a striking example. In 1958 the UN helped Lebanon, Jordan, and neighboring countries in the Middle East to settle their differences peacefully instead of by fighting. Its action in the Congo in 1960 helped keep peace and order there and perhaps saved Africa from war. The debates in the Security Council and action by the Secretary-General helped to avoid the danger of a possible nuclear war in the Cuban crisis in 1962. The Security Council sent a peace-keeping force to Cyprus and observers to Kashmir to stop the fighting there.

No on can say for sure that any of these situations would have caused a big war if it had continued. But war certainly could have resulted if the UN had not used its powerful pressures for peace.

Not only has the UN fulfilled its main purpose of keeping peace, but it has achieved several historic "firsts."

The UN Charter is itself one of the great milestones of history. It lays down rules for peaceful relations between nations. In the UN Charter, the threat or use of force is outlawed, except in self-defense or when ordered by the Security Council.

In Korea, for the first time in history, an armed invasion was halted by an international organization. The armed forces of sixteen member nations fought together under the UN flag. Again, in the Suez crisis, UNEF was the first international force ever used to bring about the peaceful withdrawal of attacking military forces.

Preventing or stopping war is the most obvious way in which the UN has proved its importance. But there are many less spectacular ways in which the UN has advanced the cause of peace and human welfare.

A sharing of economic and social gains and of scientific knowledge has been promoted all over the world. Peaceful use of atomic energy and outer space has been strongly encouraged. The UN is helping to establish the rule of law throughout the world. *Genocide*, the systematic wiping out of whole groups of people, has been declared a crime. In these and many other ways the UN is working toward the goals set by its Charter.

The Future

The UN is the only world organization equipped to deal with differences among nations. It provides the only permanent meeting place between East and West, between big and little countries, and between rich and poor ones. It is the place where the problems of the world can be explored and where the policies of all nations can be examined. Here the knowledge of all member nations can be shared and world public opinion can exert a peaceful influence.

Change is the law of life. Changes must and will take place among nations. If they do not take place peacefully, they will do so with violence and bloodshed. In a changing world, the UN not only keeps violent forces under control but actively helps to bring about peaceful changes.

In this way, under the watchful eye of the UN, there is hope that the world can develop in an orderly and peaceful manner.

Nevertheless, it is true that the UN is not a perfect organization. It has not fulfilled all the high hopes that were held for it. But in those tasks where it has not succeeded, lack of success was due largely to fear and distrust among the nations. Without the strong backing of the big powers, particularly the United States and the Soviet Union, the UN cannot achieve its goals.

The UN is a mirror of the world as it is. The sharpness of its debates is a symptom of world tension, not the cause of it. Although the UN provides the place and the means of reaching agreements, nations must also have the *will to agree*.

A carved teak wood statue, symbolizing Mankind and Hope, mounted at the north-eastern corner of the Trusteeship Council Chamber.

76

The UN Charter sets a moral standard for all nations. World public opinion works as a strong force on nations to live up to the ideals of the Charter. All nations want to win UN support for their actions.

Victor Hugo once wrote: "There is nothing in the world so powerful as an idea whose time has come." Surely the time has come for putting into action the idea of a world community, of nations joining hands to build a world of peace and plenty.

There is no more noble expression of this idea than the following:

PREAMBLE OF THE
CHARTER OF THE
UNITED NATIONS

We, the peoples of the United Nations, determined
to save succeeding generations from the scourge of war, which twice in our lifetime has brought untold sorrow to mankind, and to reaffirm faith in fundamental human rights, in the dignity and worth of the human person, in the equal rights of men and women and of nations large and small, and
to establish conditions under which justice and respect for the obligations arising from treaties and other sources of international law can be maintained, and
to promote social progress and better standards of life in larger freedom,

And for these ends
to practice tolerance and live together in peace with one another as good neighbors, and
to unite our strength to maintain international peace and security, and
to ensure, by the acceptance of principles and the institution of methods, that armed force shall not be used, save in the common interest, and
to employ international machinery for the promotion of the economic and social advancement of all peoples,

Have resolved to combine our efforts to accomplish these aims.

A Chronology of
the United Nations

1941   The Atlantic Charter is signed by President Roosevelt and Prime Minister Churchill. They declare that after the war they hope to see a permanent peace established.

1942   United Nations Declaration is signed by twenty-seven nations. They all promise to work for peace everywhere in the world when the war is over.

1944   Dumbarton Oaks Conference in Washington, D.C. Representatives of the United States, the United Kingdom, the Soviet Union, and China agree to set up a world organization for peace. The key group in this organization is to be the Security Council, in which China, France, the Soviet Union, the United Kingdom, and the United States are to have permanent seats.

1945   The United Nations Charter is signed by fifty countries in San Francisco. (Poland signed later.) The date on which the Charter came into force, October 24, now is celebrated as UN day.

1946   The first session of the General Assembly opens in London, followed shortly by the first meeting of the Security Council in that city. Trygve Lie is elected first Secretary-General. Later this year temporary headquarters of the United Nations is established at Lake Success, New York.

1947   The General Assembly adopts the flag of the United Nations.

1952   The General Assembly holds its first meeting in the new General Assembly hall at United Nations headquarters in New York City.

1953   Dag Hammarskjold is elected Secretary-General.

1961 U Thant is elected Secretary-General.
1965 The Charter is amended to increase the number of members of the Security Council from eleven to fifteen, and of the Economic and Social Council from eighteen to twenty-seven.
1970 The United Nations celebrates its twenty-fifth anniversary with the theme "Peace, justice and progress."
1971 The General Assembly votes to give the seat of China to the People's Republic of China. Kurt Waldheim is elected Secretary-General.

Special Terms

Abstention   When a member nation decides to vote neither *for* nor *against* a proposal, this is called an abstention. An abstention does not count as a vote.

Administering Authority   The nation that governs a Trust Territory.

Agenda   A list of the order of work to be taken up.

Commission   A group appointed by a senior organ for some specific work.

Committee   Same as commission.

Conciliation   The process of settling a quarrel between those involved in it, by means of a peaceful compromise. Similar to mediation.

Constitution   The basic laws of a state or of an organization.

Convention   Same as Treaty, signed by many countries.

Council   An important organ. The UN has three Councils: Security, Economic and Social, and Trusteeship.

Delegate   A member of a delegation. *See* Representative.

Delegation   A country's representatives and its staff at the UN.

Enforcement Measures   Action taken to force a country to keep the peace. Also known as sanctions.

Mediation   The process of helping those involved in a dispute to settle it by peaceful means.

Mission   *See* Delegation.

Moral Authority   The power and influence of the UN due to its prestige as an organization that represents world opinion.

Observers   Persons appointed by the UN to watch over a situation and report on activities that might cause trouble.

Organ An official main group of the UN. There are six principal organs of the UN: General Assembly, Security Council, Economic and Social Council, Trusteeship Council, International Court of Justice, and the Secretariat.

Proposal A suggestion put forward in a UN organ. Also called a draft resolution that has not yet been approved.

Representative At the UN, a person appointed to speak and act for his government. *See* Delegate.

Resolution A proposal that has been approved by a UN organ. Also called a decision.

Self-determination The right of a people to make decisions for themselves, including the decision to be independent.

Self-government The right of a people to govern themselves. Self-government does not necessarily mean independence.

Session A meeting of a UN organ, or a series of such meetings.

Sovereign State A free and independent country that is not under the rule of another country.

Technical Assistance Help given to countries in the form of technical knowledge and training, rather than in the form of money or goods.

Treaty A formal agreement between two or more countries.

Truce An armistice or an end to fighting.

Unanimity When all members vote in the same way.

Veto When a permanent member of the Security Council votes against a resolution.

List of
Member Nations

(132 as of 1972. Population in parentheses.)

Afghanistan (17,500,000)
Albania (2,200,000)
Algeria (14,800,000)
Argentina (23,500,000)
Australia (13,000,000)
Austria (7,400,000)
Bahrain (220,000)
Barbados (260,000)
Belgium (9,700,000)
Bhutan (750,000)
Bolivia (5,100,000)
Botswana (700,000)
Brazil (98,000,000)
Bulgaria (8,500,000)
Burma (28,000,000)
Burundi (3,600,000)
Byelorussian SSR (incl. in USSR)
Cameroon (5,900,000)
Canada (22,000,000)
Central African Republic (1,600,000)
Chad (3,800,000)
Chile (10,000,000)
Colombia (21,800,000)
Congo (1,000,000)
Costa Rica (1,800,000)
Cuba (8,500,000)
Cyprus (600,000)
Czechoslovakia (14,500,000)
Dahomey (2,800,000)
Denmark (5,000,000)

Dominican Republic (4,500,000)
Ecuador (6,300,000)
Egypt (34,000,000)
El Salvador (3,600,000)
Equatorial Guinea (300,000)
Ethiopia (25,000,000)
Fiji (500,000)
Finland (4,700,000)
France (51,000,000)
Gabon (500,000)
Gambia (370,000)
Ghana (9,000,000)
Greece (9,000,000)
Guatemala (5,400,000)
Guinea (4,000,000)
Guyana (800,000)
Haiti (5,000,000)
Honduras (2,700,000)
Hungary (10,400,000)
Iceland (200,000)
India (550,000,000)
Indonesia (125,000,000)
Iran (30,000,000)
Iraq (9,800,000)
Ireland (3,000,000)
Israel (3,000,000)
Italy (54,000,000)
Ivory Coast (4,400,000)
Jamaica (2,000,000)
Japan (105,000,000)

Jordan (2,400,000)
Kenya (11,700,000)
Khmer Republic (7,000,000)
Kuwait (830,000)
Laos (3,000,000)
Lebanon (2,900,000)
Lesotho (1,100,000)
Liberia (1,200,000)
Libyan Arab Republic (2,000,000)
Luxembourg (340,000)
Madagascar (7,000,000)
Malawi (4,500,000)
Malaysia (10,000,000)
Maldives (100,000)
Mali (5,000,000)
Malta (330,000)
Mauritania (1,200,000)
Mauritius (800,000)
Mexico (51,000,000)
Mongolia (1,300,000)
Morocco (16,000,000)
Nepal (11,000,000)
Netherlands (13,200,000)
New Zealand (2,900,000)
Nicaragua (2,000,000)
Niger (4,100,000)
Nigeria (57,000,000)
Norway (3,900,000)
Oman (700,000)
Pakistan (50,000,000)
Panama (1,500,000)
Paraguay (2,400,000)
People's Democratic Republic of Yemen
  (1,500,000)
People's Republic of China (800,000,000)
Peru (14,000,000)
Philippines (38,000,000)

Poland (33,000,000)
Portugal (9,700,000)
Qatar (80,000)
Romania (20,500,000)
Rwanda (3,600,000)
Saudia Arabia (6,000,000)
Senegal (4,000,000)
Sierra Leone (2,600,000)
Singapore (2,100,000)
Somalia (2,900,000)
South Africa (20,500,000)
Spain (34,100,000)
Sri Lanka (12,700,000)
Sudan (16,000,000)
Swaziland (420,000)
Sweden (8,100,000)
Syrian Arab Republic (6,500,000)
Thailand (36,000,000)
Togo (1,900,000)
Trinidad and Tobago (1,100,000)
Tunisia (5,200,000)
Turkey (36,200,000)
Uganda (10,100,000)
Ukrainian SSR (incl. in USSR)
Union of Soviet Socialist Republics
  (245,000,000)
United Arab Emirates (200,000)
United Kingdom (56,000,000)
United Republic of Tanzania (13,600,000)
United States (207,000,000)
Upper Volta (5,500,000)
Uruguay (2,900,000)
Venezuela (11,000,000)
Yemen (5,900,000)
Yugoslavia (20,600,000)
Zaïre (22,500,000)
Zambia (4,500,000)

Index

General Assembly, 5-6, 7, 10
    delegates to (*see* Delegates)
    emergency sessions of, 24-25, 38
    functions of, 14-16
    peace-keeping by, (*see* Peace-keeping)
    Presidents of, 14
    resolutions of, 14-16, 24-25
Geneva Disarmament Conference, 42-43
Great Britain. *See* United Kingdom
Great Powers, 14, 18. *See also* Veto

Hammarskjold, Dag (Secretary-General), 40, 62, 80
Human Rights, Commission on (ECOSOC), 58
Human rights, UN efforts toward, 54-55
Human Rights Day (December 10), 54
Hungarian revolt (1956), 25, 52

Indonesia:
    observers to, 31
    and Security Council, 22
International Atomic Energy Agency IAEA), 44, 60
International Bank for Reconstruction and Development (BANK), 60
International Civil Aviation Organization (ICAO), 61
International Convention on the Elimination of All Forms of Racial Discrimination (1965), 55
International Court of Justice, 10, 67-68
International Covenants on Human Rights, 54
International Finance Corporation (IFC), 60
International Labor Organization (ILO), 60, 61
International Monetary Fund (FUND), 60
International police force, 27. *See also* United Nations Emergency Force (UNEF)
International Telecommunication Union (ITU), 61
Israel:
    creation of, 35-36
    1967 war vs. Arab states, 38
    and Suez Canal, 12-13, 36
    see also Middle East crises

Jordan, and Middle East crises, 35, 38, 74

Kashmir crisis, 31, 74
Katanga province (Congo), 39
Korean War, 31, 33-34
    Secretary-General and, 41
    Security Council and, 27

Languages (official), 5-6
Latin America:
    bloc voting of, 18-19
    Economic Commission for (ECLA), 58
    nuclear weapons banned from (1967), 43
League of Nations, 7
    Mandated Territories of, 63

Lebanon:
    crisis (1958), 25, 31, 74
    and Israel, 35
Libya,
    independence for, 62

Membership:
    admission process, 14
    growth in, 9
    list of members, 84-85
Middle East crises:
    1947-49, 35-36
    1957-58, 25, 74
    1967, 38
Military forces. *See* UNEF
Mozambique, problem of, 63

Namibia (South West Africa), 63
Narcotic Drugs, Commission on (ECOSOC) 58
Netherlands, and Indonesia, 22
New Guinea, Territory of (Australia), 64
New Zealand, bloc voting of, 19
Nobel Peace Prize, 35, 51, 52, 61
Non-aligned countries, 18
Nongovernmental organizations (NGOs), 58-59
Non-Proliferation of Nuclear Weapons, Treaty for the (1968), 43
Non-Self-Governing Territories, 66
Nuclear-power reactors, 44
Nuclear weapons. *See* Disarmament

Observers (military), 31, 35
Organization of American States, 19
Outer space:
    disarmament of (1967), 43
    peaceful uses of, 44, 75
Outer Space Treaty (1967), 43

Pacific Islands, trust Territories of the (U.S.), 64
Palestine:
    1947-49 crisis, 35-36
    See also Middle East crises
Peace-keeping, 74-75
    General Assembly and, 28
    military forces and (*see* UNEF)
    military observers and, 31, 35
    Security Council and, 28
    See also: Congo; Indonesia; Korean War; Middle East crises
Population Commission (ECOSOC), 58
Portugal, African possessions of, 63
Portuguese Guinea, problem of, 63

Racism:
    in South Africa (apartheid), 55, 63
    in Southern Rhodesia, 63
    UN efforts vs., 55
Refugees, 52
    Arab, 36